Maurice Ravel

MOTHER GOOSE

5 Children's Pieces

version for solo piano by Lawrence Rosen
and original version for piano four-hands

cover design by Edith E. Newman

ED-4000
First Printing: December 1995

G. SCHIRMER, *Inc.*

7777 W. BLUEMOUND RD. P.O. BOX 13819 MILWAUKEE, WI 53213

MOTHER GOOSE
5 Children's Pieces

I. Sleeping Beauty's Pavane

Maurice Ravel
(1875 – 1937)
version for solo piano by Lawrence Rosen

II. Tom Thumb

He thought he'd have no trouble finding his way back by following the breadcrumbs he'd left everywhere he'd gone; how surprised he was when he couldn't find a single one; the birds had come and eaten them all. (Ch. Perrault)

pp
cresc.
f molto espr.
p
mf

8va
pp
p espr.
pp
pp espr.
pp
poco rit.

III. Little Miss Ugly Face, Empress of the Pagodas

She undressed and got in her bath. Immediately, the denizens of the pagodas began singing and playing their instruments: some had theorbos made of chestnut shells; others had viols made of almond shells; for their instruments were necessarily proportional to their own size. (Mme. d'Aulnoy: Green Streamers)

March tempo ♩ = 116

8va
pp
p
f
pp
p

p
gliss.
10
pp
cresc.
(cresc.)
ff
8va
f
f
pp
espr.

ppp
pp molto espr.
3
p
3
p

3
pp espr.
ppp senza espr.
mf
p

8va
f
pp
p
8va
pp
f
p
pp
p
mf

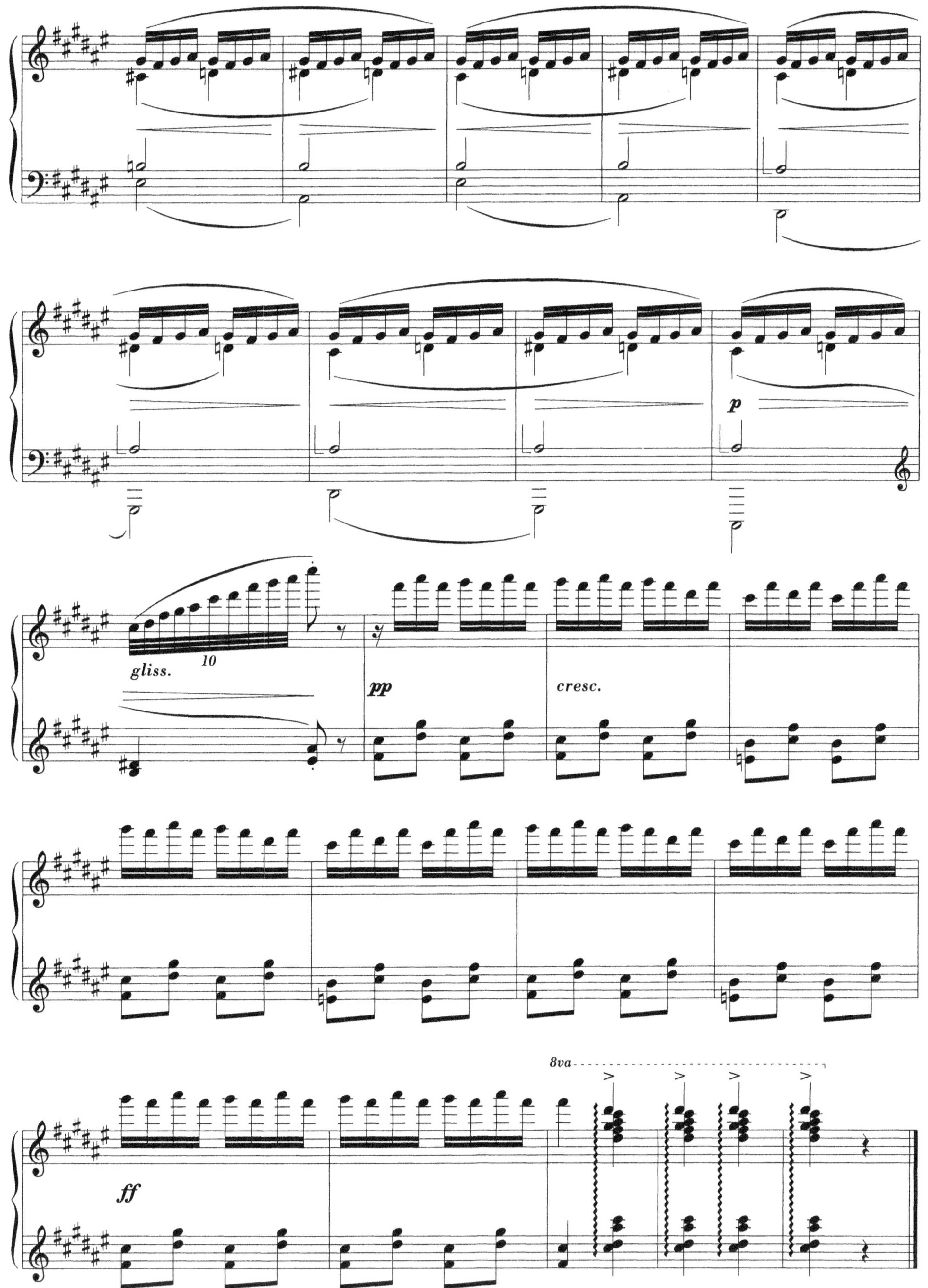

gliss.
10
p
pp
cresc.
ff
8va

IV. Conversations between the Beauty and the Beast

"When I think of your kind heart, you don't seem so ugly."—"Oh my yes, I have a kind heart, but I'm hideous."—"Many men are more hideous than you."—"If I had wit, I'd think of a fine compliment to thank you, but I'm only a beast."

"Beauty, will you marry me?"—"No, Beasty!"

"I'll die happy, since I've had the pleasure of seeing you again."—"No, Beasty dear, you shan't die: you will live and be my husband." . . . The Beast vanished, and at her feet she now found a prince more handsome than love itself, who thanked her for breaking the spell that bound him. (Mlle. Leprince de Beaumont)

p

pp

ppp

very short

pp

un poco marc.

p

pp

mf

p

pp

pp
p molto espr.
pp
accel. poco a poco
p
p
mf
sempre cresc.
Very lively
rall.
f
ff

Tempo I
pp
poco marc.
pp
p
f
accel. poco a poco
cresc. poco a poco
Lively
ff

8va
pp
gliss.
espr.
cresc.
loco
p
dim.
rall.
Slower
8va
pp
p
espr.
poco marc.
rall.
L.H.
ppp

V. The Magic Garden

8va
pp
pp cresc.
(loco)
rit.
f dim.
a tempo
pp
poco cresc.
p cresc.
8va
gliss.
l.h.
ff

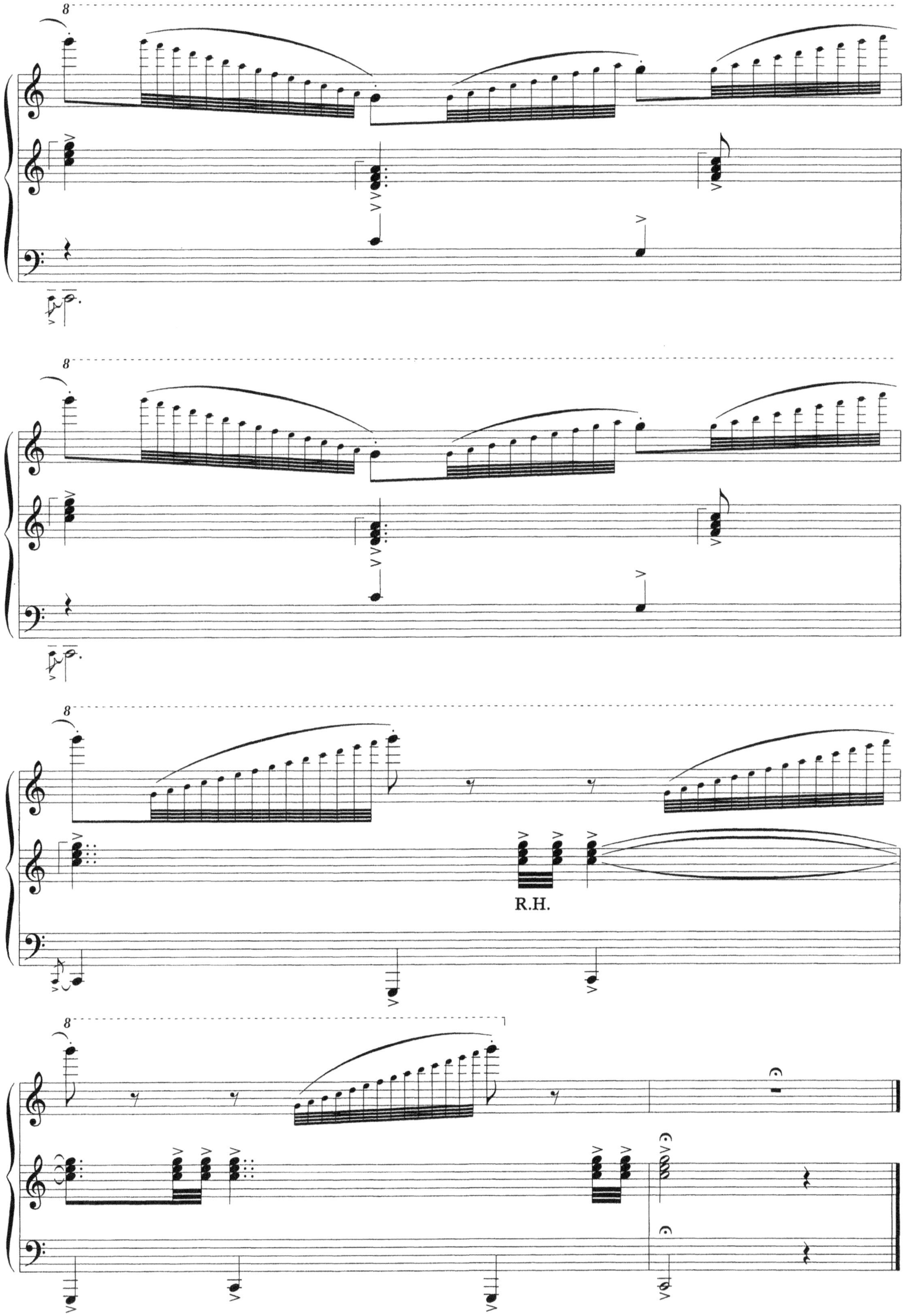

8
8
8
R.H.
8

MOTHER GOOSE

5 Children's Pieces

Maurice Ravel

I. Sleeping Beauty's Pavane

MOTHER GOOSE

5 Children's Pieces

Maurice Ravel

I. Sleeping Beauty's Pavane

II. Tom Thumb

He thought he'd have no trouble finding his way back by following the breadcrumbs he'd left everywhere he'd gone; how surprised he was when he couldn't find a single one; the birds had come and eaten them all. (Ch. Perrault.)

II. Tom Thumb

He thought he'd have no trouble finding his way back by following the breadcrumbs he'd left everywhere he'd gone; how surprised he was when he couldn't find a single one; the birds had come and eaten them all. (Ch. Perrault.)

PRIMA

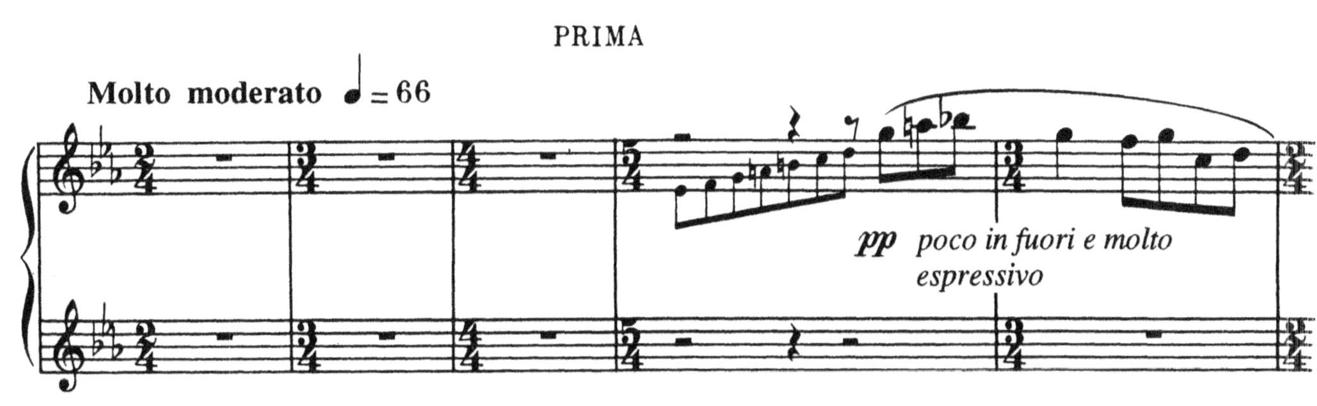

pp
pp
f
molto espressivo
3
p
mf

pp
pp
f molto espressivo
3
p
3
mf

in fuori ed espressivo
p
pp
pp
m.s. espressivo
pp
Poco ritenuto

8
pp
espressivo
Poco ritneuto

III. Little Miss Ugly Face, Empress of the Pagodas

She undressed and got in her bath. Immediately, the denizens of the pagodas began singing and playing their instruments: some had theorbos made of chestnut shells; others had viols made of almond shells; for their instruments were necessarily proportioned to their own size. (Mme. d'Aulnoy: Green Streamers)

SECONDA

III. Little Miss Ugly Face, Empress of the Pagodas

She undressed and got in her bath. Immediately, the denizens of the pagodas began singing and playing their instruments: some had theorbos made of chestnut shells; others had viols made of almond shells; for their instruments were necessarily proportioned to their own size. (Mme. d'Aulnoy: Green Streamers)

PRIMA

pp
p
p
8
Ped.
*
pp
ff

pp
p
gliss.
8
pp
8
ff

f
pp
espressivo
pp
p

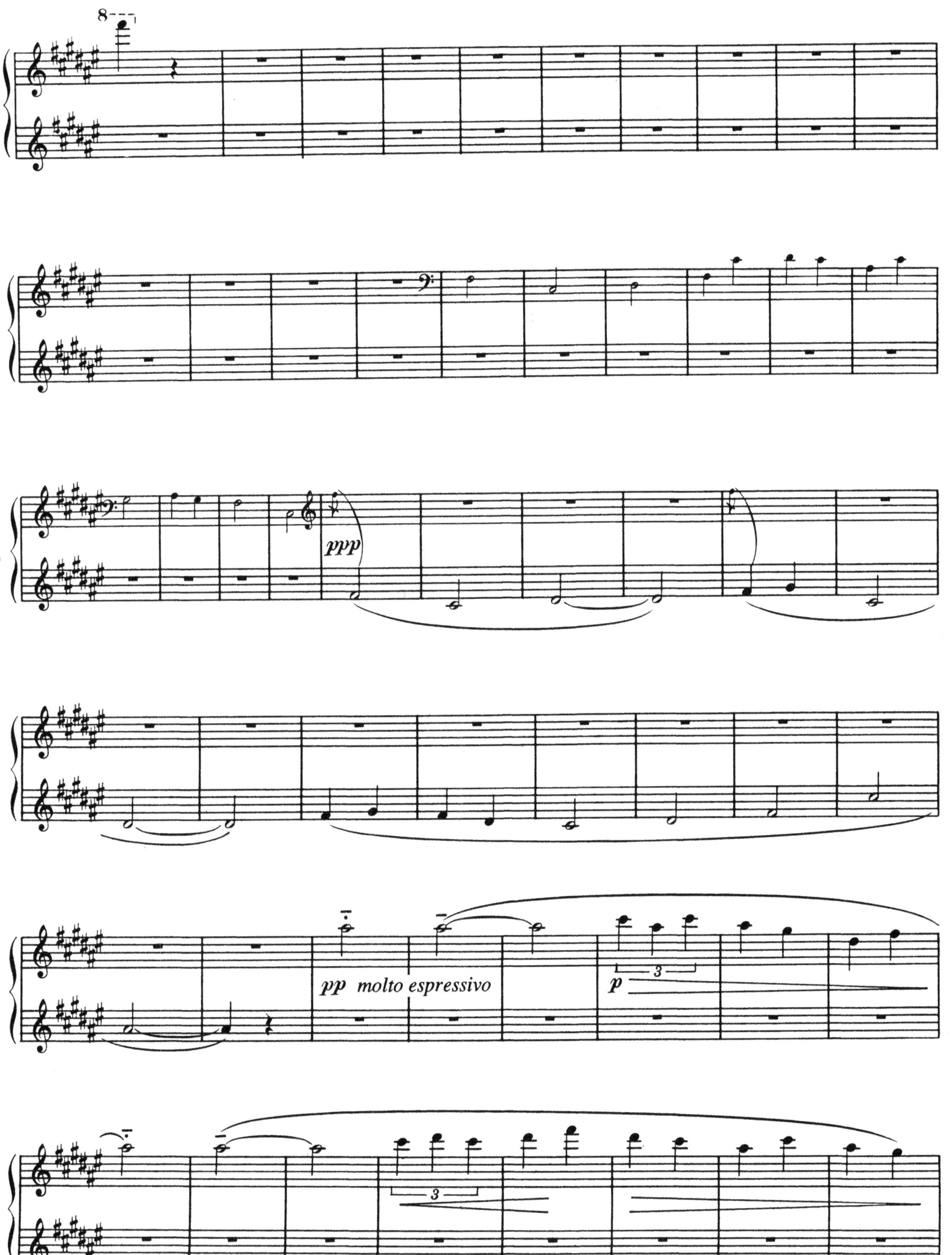
8
ppp
pp molto espressivo
3
p
3

p
pp
in fuori ed espressivo
mf
p
f
p
f
p
f

p
ppp senza espress.
f
pp
f
pp
f

pp
p
mf
p
8
Ped.
pp
ff

pp
p
gliss.
p
8
pp
8
ff

IV. Conversations between the Beauty and the Beast

"When I think of your kind heart, you don't seem so ugly."—"Oh my yes, I have a kind heart, but I'm hideous."—"Many men are more hideous than you."—"If I had wit, I'd think of a fine compliment to thank you, but I'm only a beast."

....

"Beauty, will you marry me?"—"No, Beasty!"

....

"I'll die happy, since I've had the pleasure of seeing you again."—"No, Beasty dear, you shan't die: you shall live and be my husband."...The Beast vanished, and at her feet she now found a prince more handsome than love itself, who thanked her for breaking the spell that bound him. (Mlle. Leprince de Beaumont)

SECONDA

IV. Conversations between the Beauty and the Beast

"When I think of your kind heart, you don't seem so ugly."—"Oh my yes, I have a kind heart, but I'm hideous."—"Many men are more hideous than you."—"If I had wit, I'd think of a fine compliment to thank you, but I'm only a beast."

....

"Beauty, will you marry me?"—"No, Beasty!"

....

"I'll die happy, since I've had the pleasure of seeing you again."—"No, Beasty dear, you shan't die: you shall live and be my husband."...The Beast vanished, and at her feet she now found a prince more handsome than love itself, who thanked her for breaking the spell that bound him. (Mlle. Leprince de Beaumont)

molto breve
p
pp
ppp
pp
p un poco in fuori
(U.C.)
p
pp
mf
p
pp
pp
pp

molto breve
pp
p
p
molto espressivo
p
pp
8

Animando
poco
a
poco
p
p
Vivo assai
f
Rall.
Tempo I
ff
pp
un poco in fuori
pp
p

Animando poco a poco
p
mf
Vivo assai
f
Rall.
ff
Tempo I
pp
pp
p

Animando poco a
poco
Vivo
ff
pp
Rall.
p
pp
Quasi lento
p espressivo ed in fuori
Rall.
ppp

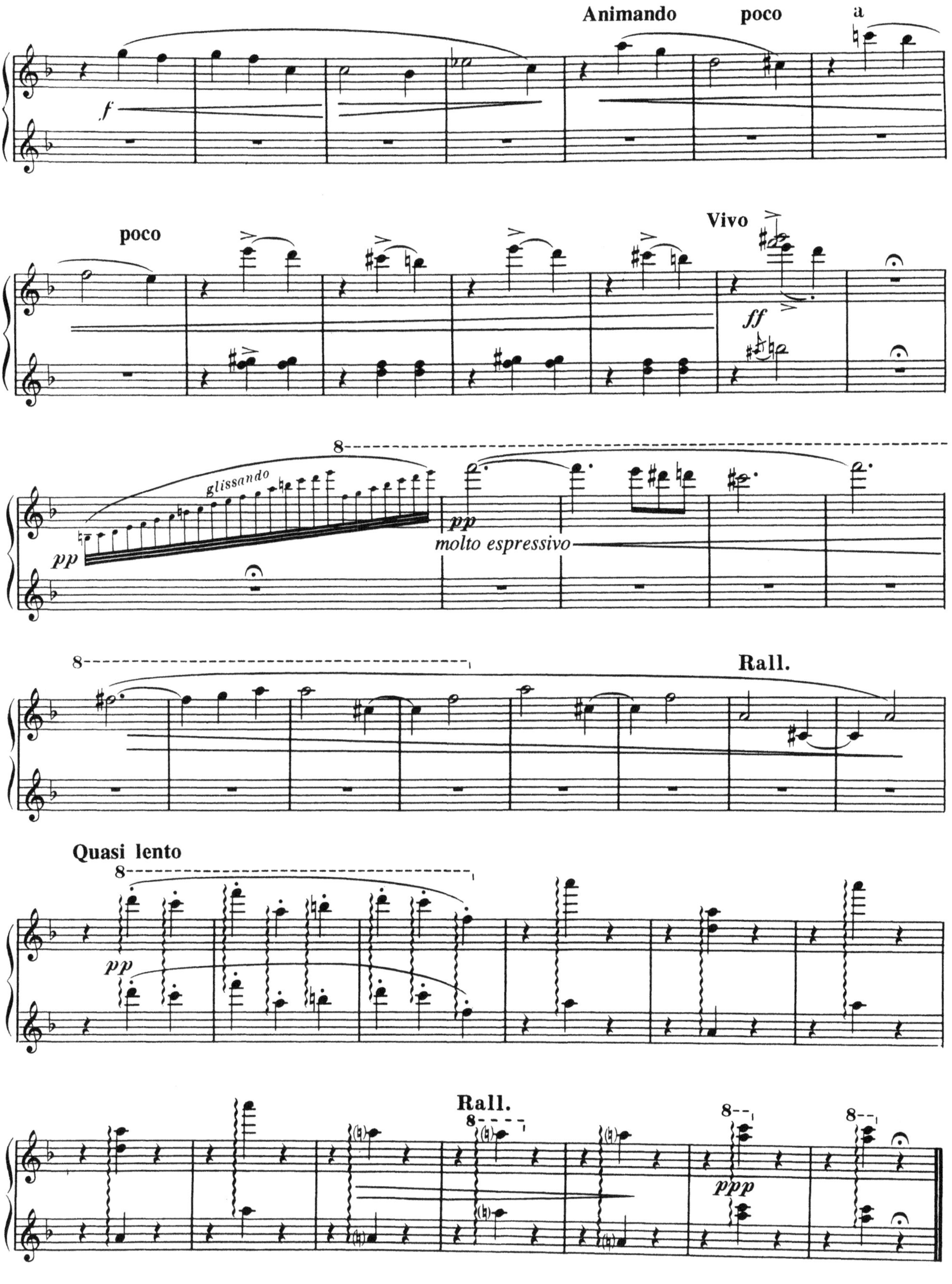

PRIMA
Animando
poco
a
f
poco
Vivo
ff
8
glissando
pp
pp
molto espressivo
8
Rall.
Quasi lento
8
pp
Rall.
8
8
8
ppp

V. The Magic Garden

SECONDA

V. The Magic Garden

pp
f

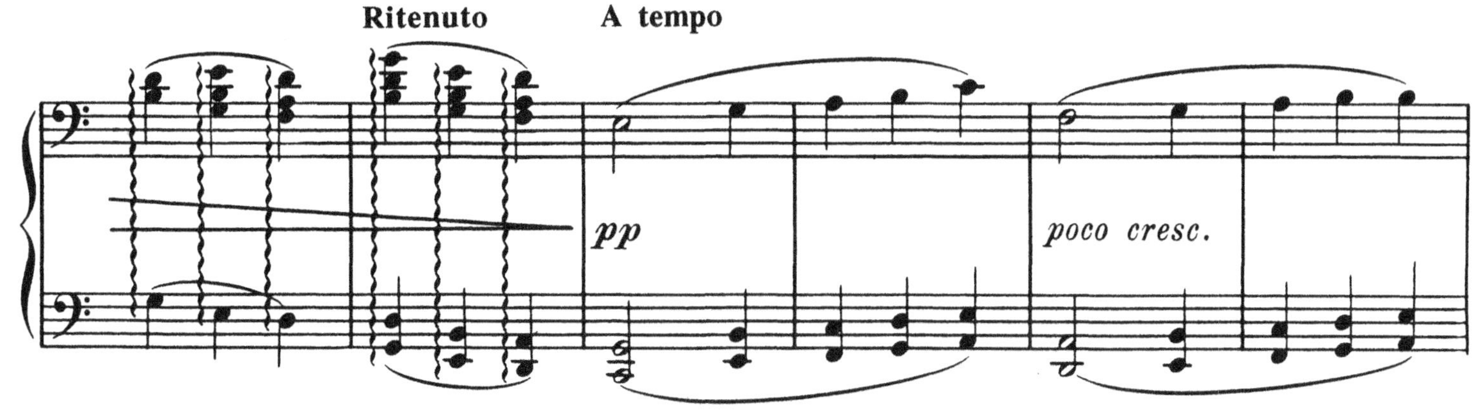
Ritenuto
A tempo
pp
poco cresc.

p

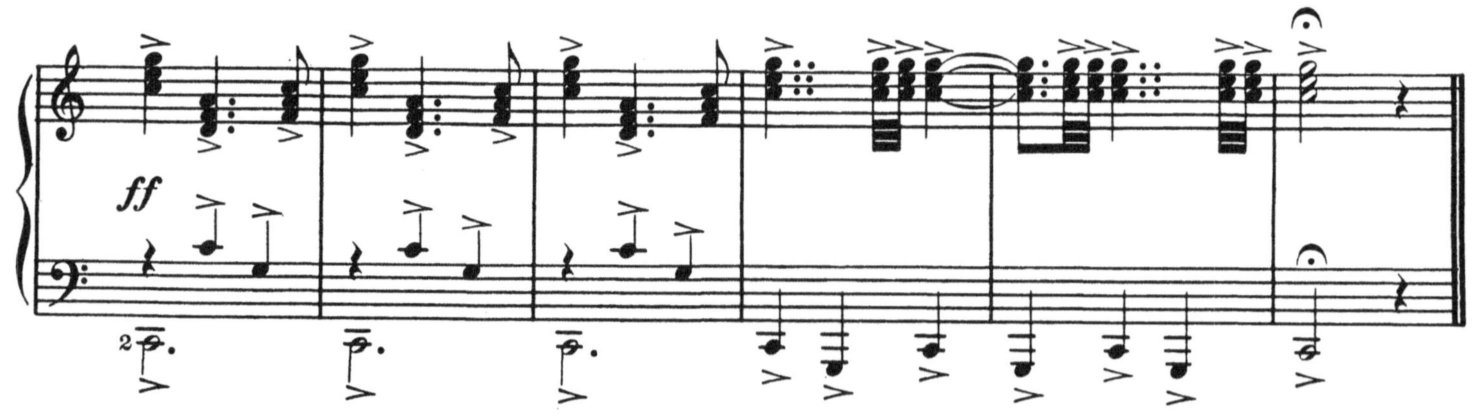
ff

Ritenuto
A tempo
pp
f
pp
poco cresc.
p
ff
glissando